Soul Mates in the Moonlight

By Terry Jeff

Title Picture

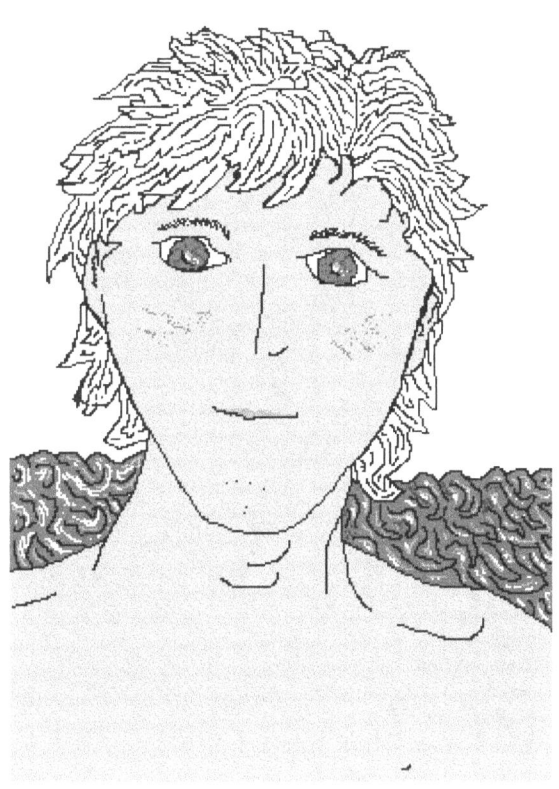

Copyright 2012 Terry Jeff

Your ISBN: 978-1-105-73153-2

Soul Mates in the Moonlight

Chapter 1
Love starts with a smile.

"Love starts with a smile, grows with a kiss, and ends with a tear." he said to me. I stared across the computer screen knowing all too well those words were etched in my soul. My heart ached since the last time, we had could talked together online.

It was like heaven had brought us together to be as one. We would type for hours on end sending messages back and forth. Sometimes he wrote at the same time I did. It was uncanny the number occasions that would happen. It only reinforced the belief that we were meant for each other.

The moonlight was drifting in through the window, as I continued to chat. It moved across the floor to the bed with the white sheets.

It felt like he was there with me talking that first night, as if I had known him all my life. He understood my needs, wants, fears, failures, and even my successes for some reason. How could that be possible from the other side of the world? He comprehended me then and continues to do so today.

I still recall those words we spoke that day we met in person six months ago.

We are now brothers: I was eighteen years with the black hair, the blue eyes, and the build of a high school wrestling senior in a small town community. Everyone called me Tee for short. However, he was only younger in years to me at 18 with blond hair and blue eyes. And, he played rugby and tennis.

From the very first day that we met we called each other. However, no one expected little brother and big brother. However, no one expected that we would continue chatting for such a long period of time.

My chat partner took his first rugby test today to see if he could qualify for the senior boys team. It is like a beep test. My friend needed to race to a designated point. Then, he had to rush back. He runs to a point. And he runs back.

"This is for rugby?" I asked

He nodded his head and looking into my ocean blue eyes and replied carefully,

"Running to a point and back is easy."

He laughed at me and continued, "I am not yet done talking to you! Be quit! You run to a further point, and then you return. Repeat the lap, all while being timed. When you exceed, when you drop below the limit you have to stop. I did eight circuits today! The record is ten!

"Not bad for a young pup like you!"

I rubbed his shoulders while gazing into those deep blue eyes of his once more, as he spoke about the test.

"Yep! One guy even fertilized the yard a little!" he smirked. "Well, if I did that I would be puking from the strain of that entire run. By God!... Watching the complete race could be exhausting! But, looking at you is never tiresome!"

As I observed him more closely, I replied, as I looked at him closer saying these words to him.

 "Yes, the running is a killer. But, you have to do some things in life that may not make sense at the time."

He pinched me, as he said that.

"Stop! That hurts!"

"That's the point!... Life does hurt sometimes!"

 As we talked that first time, which for me was night that first night him was morning that stretched into his afternoon, because we were on different hours and him in his afternoon hours because we are on the opposite sides of the world, our lives began to change for the both of us.

 We shared secrets that neither one had revealed to anyone else. A secret world that was hidden even from ourselves. But, on that night we trusted each other and we talked and cried our eyes out until we could no longer read the screen.

It was precisely, then, that I knew I was falling in love with this person who lived across the other side of the world from me. How could that be? All we had to go on was written words: his and mine! We saw no pictures of each other: Just a trust in our conversation and the bonding of the spirit that brings people together.

I remembered role-playing the scene of little and big brother. I had no real little younger sibling, but here was someone to talk to and confide in.   A person to whom was someone I could talk too. This was someone I would be able to tell my deepest secrets. Someone I could guide in life through all the ups and downs, because I had already been there.

We discussed our horrible pasts: the nights of being beaten and being raped by a relative or someone else. We talked of getting thrown out of our house and another relative taking us in to be their son.

We discussed ways to end the abuse that was going on in our lives, and which had caused so much pain. We proposed means to change our lives. How to stop the anger deep within ourselves before it would rage out of control. No one knew the anger deep inside us when it rages out and no one but us could really know, because we are being sexually abused by a guy who threatened to kill us if we tell anybody.

How can we tell others?... What will our friends think once they find out we have been raped, made to swallow stuff we never thought we would, forced to put our lips on places they were never meant to be?

We chatted about lying down together in bed while holding and comforting one another, as we talked and cried.

Sometimes just cuddling and kissing is all that is needed. This was something that everyone deserves: to be held and told they are needed by someone not to be used and abused!

The computer screen glistened it lights from the moonlight spreading across the room. We are lying down in bed. The crickets are chirping loudly.   They can be heard, as the breeze blows through the window.

White crisp sheet are on the bed. The white crisp sheets were on the bed fresh smelling like our bodies that lie under them. I can see his blond hair resting on the pillow: My little brother, as I called him. I recline next to my

friend the warmth of his body against mine. My arm encircles his upper torso: holding him, knowing him, caressing his chest with my finger tips' as he moans and pushes back into me.

He turns looking into my face and smiles. The moonlight sparkles off of his teeth, and I can see the top of his muscular chest exposed to the light. My finger slid across his upper body, as his deep blue eyes look into mine.

It is as if the ocean from his side of the world came crashing into my corner of the earth. My fingers continue their journey sliding down his abdomen along ridges exploring and exposing areas I was unsure to touch on his torso. He moaned looking up at me. Then my friend leans in to kiss me gently on my lips.

I return his gesture, but with great ardor! I push with passion on his lips. My tongue moved in, while he explores mine. My hand slides down, urgently exploring his hot body and kissing. Our eyes remain closed with our hands clasped.

We wanted each other. We knew that from the moment we first talked proceeding with the love from that fateful day. It was now how do we do this with love that we had already built into our relationship. Can my lover and I remain united when so many other fail? How do we stay together when so many people fall apart in their attempts at lasting love?

We finally pull away while breathing hard and gazing into each looking into each other's eyes.

"I love you, little brother."

He looked up with those deep blue eyes twinkling from the moon light and whispered into my ear,

"I love you!... You will never know how much."

I said! "I realize and you have any idea how long I waited for a little brother just so I can look after them. Someone I could talk too. A person who cares about me, and I can care about them. A friend to share my emotions, hurts, feelings and experiences with for as long as time will allow us to do so"

"You know I wanted to make love to you." I said as he nodded his head.

"I would let you, because I know it is love."

I search his eyes, and I can tell in my heart he would die for me. I look at him reclining on the white sheets with my arm under his head: the blond hair lying in all directions.

He scoots closer to me, put his head upon my chest and laid down his hand upon my upper biceps. I felt his hip against my leg with his upper leg resting on mine. One hand reaches up holding his upper back and my other hand touches his knee that was on my body. Soon I hear his breathing begin get rested and mine also does as the moonbeams tripping went across the floor to our bed.

I awake the next morning and my arms were wrapped with a pillow. This can't be had I dream this? I know I felt that we talked the night away; we kissed and said we love each other, but he is gone! The curtains are closed. The window shut and locked. I step on a pair of red briefs. I still have my blue ones on!

The computer screen is blinking a message.

"Big brother, I love you. You are so special to me that you never will know. You have helped me get through a rough moment when my life was at its lowest. I can't tell you now but sometimes in the future I will. I left something on the floor for you."

I look down: It was the red silky briefs that he wore. Unconsciously, I pick them up, bring the undies to my face and smell them. The underpants are his no doubt!

I turn to the computer and begin to type,

"Little brother, oh mate, you left me something! Since you logged off your computer I will return them when we meet. And, little one, you better be ready: Tonight, my love is all yours!

Soul Mates in the Moonlight

Chapter 2

Tonight is for you.

The next night the computer screen was blinking again. It emitted light shining across the room. Suddenly. A message flashed came across the screen.

"Tonight is your night Big Brother! I'm all yours!"

I had taken his red silky briefs and, put them on and hid mine under my lover's pillow: The place where he would rest his head when he returned that night.

The glistening moon emitted rays that entered the room and advanced across the floor until it reached the bed. This action caused my heart to beat faster.

I must have fallen asleep, because the next thing I knew was feeling someone getting into my bed. I must have fallen asleep because the next moment I felt the bed move as if someone sat on it and got in. I turned looking at his smooth sexy torso, his blues eyes and his long blond hair that fell around his face. I gazed down! With his grin as he pulled the sheet up and could tell he was naked. His grin radiating in the moonlight I reached up and ran my fingers along the edge of his chin.

"I see you like wearing my red briefs, Tee!"

My boy friend held up the cover just a little to look down the length of my hard body lying next to him.
The red silky undies clung tightly to my hips. They tautly stretched over my hardness, because his affect on me.
There was 'nearly' insufficient material to contain my excitement: almost not enough.

I looked up grinning and told him to reach under his pillow for a surprise. My boy friend searched and, then, the sexy, silky and blue briefs. They had been mine! He lifted the briefs to his nose and smelled them. A great big smile spread across his face. He leaned over and gently pressed his lips against mine. Searching my mouth and licking my chin with his tongue, my Little Brother repeatedly kissed my earlobes. His tongue searching my mouth and licking my chin with kisses, down to my earlobes he kissed then he continued his journey on down my neck. Then biting a little on the ears and down my neck. I moaned feeling his hard wetness against my side and his tongue along my neck. He said,

"Hold on a moment."

My man reached down to the edge of the bed pulling something over his toes and up his strong muscular legs. He arched his body off the bed of the mattress, stretching the object over and pulled it over his hips.

"There!... That feels better!"

Holding up the sheets, I glanced down at his hairless torso to see what he just done. My lover had my blue silky briefs! Licking my lips I gazed at his ocean blue eyes and said, "Oh, that looks better!"

My friend reached out and grabbed my fingers in his right hand pulling them to his chest. Then, he intertwined them with his fingers. We laid like that for a long time talking about school: classes were going better for both of us. My boy turned and looked me in the eyes and kissed me gently on the lips.

Then, he said; "The reason I am having a good year is because of you, Big Brother. You have helped me through some hard times and have kept me focused on what I need to do in my life! You will never know how much of you an aid you are to me!"

A tear rolled down his face splashing into my cheek. My eyes welled up hearing and feeling it drop onto the pillow.

I reached up grabbing him tightly to my body and feeling him start to tremble as he cried on my shoulder. My pillow and upper body became wet: not from grief but from the happiness that we had found.

I whispered into his ear,

"I believe you are able to do anything in your life! You can be whatever your heart desires yourself to be. You need to forget the past, but you don't have to forgive the people you took away your innocence! However you do need to go on!"

I looked up into his face at him, as his eyes twinkled in the moonlight. Tears rolled down his face. My lover kissed gently on the lips, saying!

"You know you can have me Tee! I am yours to do with in any way you want me! Because I want to give myself to you!"

I wiped away a tear from his cheek with the back of my hand as it moved through his long blond hair.

"Little Brother: I also realize you want me! However, tonight we just need to hold onto what we have together, because one never knows what tomorrow will bring. I love you so much my heart aches when we are unable to talk, to listen to each other to or to touch each other in our lives together."

My hand rubbed his shoulder and upper back feeling his strong muscles as his body lay on top of me. My partner's hairless thigh was pressed against the hot skin of my hip. I could feel him against my hips, his smooth upper hairless thigh across me pressing down against my hot skin. I knew that this sexual ecstasy could not last. However, I wanted much more from our relationship than I had experienced from others in the past!

Brother, I have learned that we need someone to love, or we are lost! You are the one I want in my life! You have banished the darkness I felt for so long and replace it with eternal light!"

"It is as if the sun shines every hour in my life."

I needed to say that to him no matter how he might have felt.

"Big Brother, you are my inspiration, my role model, and my shining star! I can only hope to be the best just for you! You're the older sibling that God forgot to give me" he whispered.

My body began to burn with a fire so intense that my skin felt searing to the touch. My little brother noticed the heat and I leaned up looking down my body. My chest rose and fell as I sobbing more intensely than I ever had in the past. Short crying sounds escaped my mouth. In response, my Little Bro laid his head down on my chest holding onto my bicep with one hand while his other head my head tightly against his face.

"Big brother, listen to me! I mean it! You are my inspiration to do better every day at school! I have never worked this hard before in my life! You provide me with the desire to improve, because you care about me. I look up to you as my role model, someone I can come to for advice! You are my shining star. I will love you for the rest of eternity."

"Little One, I glad I am not your planet, Uranus."

"Why, thank you! But, I do like your Uranus: You know that! It is a lot better than Pluto!"

I grinned at him.

"My love, it is for you to use anytime you want!"

"Yep, but I like your rings around Saturn better any day of the week!"

"I prefer yours as well."

My amour laughed, as he repeated it to me.

"But what I like the best is the full moon to observe over the night sky or in bed. I am thinking of you when I fall asleep! I know you see the same bright body in the sky, as I do."

"Earth's satellite watches over two of the best brothers the world could ever have on the planet. Here to take care of you and me for as long as it shines down upon us!"

In that moment I felt tired, because of all the emotions we had gone through from crying to laughing to caring so deeply for each other.

The moonlight filled the room as we lay on the crisp white coverings. I inhaled the freshness of the sheets while we snuggled next to each other. I smelled the odor, as it combined from our sheets and bodies. A new scent was being generated from the heat of our inner beings as our colognes merges into one. I am sure when I wake up it will still linger in the air and on me.

Soul Mates in the Moonlight

Chapter 3

Opening Up to Each Other

I want to let our readers know this is our story and how we have met and been together for a long time.

The computer screen blinked the message: "I will be there tonight when the moon is high in the sky. I really must speak to you and be held by you!"

I replied: "I can talk to you now if you want."

No response was forthcoming. However, I left the monitor on, allowing it to glow across the room.

The wind blew hard against the curtains causing them to flap and my eyes to slowly close. I tried to stay awake by watching the computer screen, but that only made it worse. My breathing was slow and silent, as I lay on the top of the sheets. The moonlight gradually drifted across the floor to the edge of the bed. It touched my foot and sent an energy jolt soaring through my body like I had never before experienced in my life.

Suddenly, I felt the wetness of a kiss on my foot! I awoke immediately and turned facing my little brother. He was knelling at the end of the bed waiting for the moonshine to cross the sheets. Scooting up to the edge I took my lover in my arms. We stood in the light together. I could feel a bolt of energy surging through both of us at that moment. I gazed into his face, then he kissed me on my lips. My hands drifted down to his ass cheeks pressing him into me, as we looked into each other's blue eyes.

His eyes welled up, and a tear rolled down his cheek.

"Little Brother what's wrong tonight?!"

I held him in my arms and rocked him, as the wind blew around our bodies sending tornado like dust clouds swirling under the bed and throughout the room.

"I need to tell you more about me. Big Brother, will you hold me, as we talk tonight?"

"Yes!"

I clutched him him tightly to my chest.

"I hate my parents!... I despise them with all my heart!"

"What have they done to you at home?"

"No!^Å Tee, I never told you I was adopted at the age often by my uncle and aunt. They took me in when no one else would."

"Oh!... I see! Are you talking about your real parents, or the ones who adopted you now?"

"Big Brother," he paused.

His hand gripped my biceps and, then, slid down to my fingers grasping them in a prayer shaped form. I held on tightly and waited.

"Whenever you want to talk go ahead!" Å I am in no hurry!"

"Tonight, will you hold me and never let me go?! I don't want to lose you! Sometimes being the only child, I am lonely! I have got lots of friends, but no big brother like you to talk to me, to hold me and to NOT abuse me!"

I listened to him and watched his blue eyes blinking like ocean waves breaking onto the shore.

"Big Brother, when I was little my parents use to beat me all the time! They both got drunk and hit me! I tried to hide, but they always found me! Then, the cycle would start all over again!

"Little Brother, I am listening!... And, I am here for you!"

"Sometimes, I am so angry I want to explode! I can't help myself! I count to ten. Then, I beat my pillow! Occasionally, I cry so much that the pillow gets too wet for me to rest my head on."

My arms held him while stroking his blond hair and pulling it back from his face.

"My parents beat me so badly that I had bruises! This caused excessive amount of hatred to build up within me. It began to eat me alive! I didn't know how to control it! until I decided to play rugby. An added benefit from participating in the game was the alibi it gave me to explain my injuries. No one would be able to tell the difference. I lived a lie: I hated being deceitful every day of my life!"

"I bet it was hard to go through!" Sometimes it's better to let it all go!"

"Yes!" ÅI felt like killing myself!"

"Once they hurt me so badly that I broke both my arm and collar bone!"

"I thought you might have been hurt, but I wasn't sure. Did the authorities step in and help?"

"Yeah! But, I tried to cover it up thinking it was my fault! Then, I got in trouble with the law! My real parents said I was a little shit, and the officials believed them! Later on, my aunt and uncle took me in: Fortunately, they are real strict about everything! I think I needed that, because without their guidance I wouldn't have made it!"

"Little Brother, I am glad you are here today! You are an important person with real value! Don't let anyone ever take that away from you!

He squeezed my hand, as I said that to him.

"The night my arm got broken, I stood outside in the dark for a long time. I didn't know what to do! I walked to my aunt and uncle's house and told them what has been going on for a long time. It was cold and raining that night. I had to go two miles!"

"Little Bro, you went two miles with a broken limb?!"

He nodded towards me. I could only tighten my hold around his shoulder, as he laid his head on me.

"My love,^Å I knew something bad had to have happened at home, at school or where ever: Right?!"

I felt him tremble: A cold chill ran through both our bodies at the same time!

I waited.

"Yes!"Å I kept thinking about what happened to me! I have read about when people abuse you, you often grow up to be an abuser as well!"

"Little Brother, have you told a counselor about these feeling! You know that it is important to see a professional. They can help you sort out your emotions and guide you to find the right direction!"

"But, I have you now Big Brother to aid me!"

"I understand what you are saying, and I will always be here for you any time you're are having troubles! However, I am suggesting that you see someone."

"I know!" Å But, I am much better, since I have a big brother! You made me improve for you.

"No!" You need to do this for YOURSELF not for me! I will be here watching, listening, and cheering you on. I expect a good report card when that time comes! Alright?!"

He laughed for the first time. Then, he looked up at me and said,

"I want you yo know that you are the first person outside of my family that I have told this to! Tee, I really trust you!"

"I am honored that you are confiding in me! However, it is important that you keep talking to others, my love! You may be able to help someone else in the future! There a lot of bad things that happen to people out there! The world can be a really evil or good place. Some kids aren't as fortunate as you were. Even if your parents right now are so strict with you. Someday you will look back and thank God they helped get you through all of this."

I sat there crying, as I said these words to him. And, I sensed my shirt was wet from his tears where he had laid his head on my shoulder talking the night away.

"Are you all right, Little Brother?"

"Yes, I feel much better."

"I had to tell you. I wanted you to know. Tee,... there is more, but I can't say it!"

"That is fine!... When you are ready I will listen! You know that just as the sun rises in the morning and the moon at night so shall I be here for you!"

My hand held him tightly, as we lay half on and half off the bed. Our legs draped over the edge touching the floor, and our upper bodies hugged, as if protecting each other from whatever danger lurked beyond the doors.

The wind blew the curtains with great force throughout the night, as the moon's light crept across the bed. Silence filled the room. Our breathing, slow and shallow, was the only thing heard. Sometime during the night I felt the bed move, but I didn't awaken. The next morning, while I was still laying in the same spot that I had fallen asleep in, I looked at the edge of the bed. It was empty!

The computer screen was blinking. I got up reading the message.

"Thank you Tee for being there for me last night. You were awesome in helping me make a decision!

Soul mates in the Moonlight

Chapter 4

The story you are reading is ours. Specifically, it is about our life growing up and about how we found each other. Little Brother is Jeff and Big Brother is Terry.

   I checked the computer hoping for a message from my little brother and wondering if Jeff was all right. Suddenly, my computer screen went dead. I had no power, so I left it on and crawled into bed. I looked out of my window and saw the moonlight creep through the backyard tree.

   I drifted to sleep only to be awakened by a touch on my leg, as my lover's fingers massaged my inner thighs. In response, I spread my limbs apart feeling the smoothness of the skin-on-skin contact. I opened my eyes to see Jeff sitting on the edge of the bed in his red briefs.

   My body, deeply sun-tanned from swimming all summer, lay naked under the white sheets. I moaned to his touch.

"Shhhhh. Big Brother I am here for you tonight! I am at your command to do to me whatever you so desire!"

   I felt him move up. His skin touched mine, Our lips caressed gently, as my fingers rubbed his sun-darkened back. My hands snaked down to his tight red briefs cupping them while pressing his crotch into mine. I could feel his little boy's stiffness lying next to my naked shaft. We kept up the kissing and cuddling for ten minutes, as he slowly moved down my body. During my beloved's journey he licked my chin and neck wet with his tongue. His fingers stretched out across my chest touching my nipples.

   I moaned again, as they hardened to his touch. I had wanted this so much from him, but I was unsure how far he would go with me! My fingers intertwined with his hair, as he looked up into my blue eyes. I could see him surfing my body, as his tongue moved down to my belly button.

   I squirmed under all the attention I was getting from my little brother.

'If this is a dream let it last forever', I thought to myself.

But, then, how could it be a dream when I felt the wetness and the heat of his body pressed against mine.

"Terry, this is for you tonight!"

The moon shone brightly across the bed, as I saw his figure crouched over my inclined body. He took my hard cock into his hand and stroked it. His erotic motions caused me to gasp and moan. My back arched off the bed wanting more of my prick to be explored by his diminutive manipulating fingers.

   The bed shifted in reaction to his muscular upper legs spreading my thighs apart.. I then felt him kiss the tip of my hard-reddened cock. He lapped around the head again and again. Then, Jeff traveled down on one side of the shaft and came back up the other. His little smooth tongue licking all over my hard dick.. I could feel his hairless legs spreading my thighs even farther apart, as he scooted down to tongue my balls and stroke my hard shaft.

   "Jeff, you feel so good!... And, this is so right!"

"Big Brother, this is your night!... I am here for you!"

   Jeff went back to bobbing up and down on my shaft, as his clenched hand jacked me, The other one journeyed up toward my chest touching my left nipple: He squeezed it hard!
   "AAAAAAAAAhhhhhhh!!" I moaned loudly arching my back into his hand and mouth.

While holding his head with one of my hands, I used the fingers on the other to grasp his strawberry blond hair. Meanwhile, he moved faster and sucked harder on my cock. As a result, I arched higher getting more of my dick into his small hot mouth.

"Jeff, my little one, you don't have to swallow it!... Just jack me off!"

However, he ignored my request and kept up the speed and suction! I rolled my head from side to side, while my eyes seemed to turn inward. I squeezed my ass cheeks together pushing my hips upward.

A volcanic like explosion burst forth from my cock: not just once but several times! Powerful spurts burst into his mouth, as my little brother hungrily devoured all my love juice. Then, he finished his labor of love by cleaning me up.

 "It's my time to return the favor!"

  "No need to!"

I reached down to his red briefs: They were soaking wet in the front! He had cum several times!

 "Oh!..., I feel.!..."

I pulled Jeff up to my side and wrapped my arms around him! Then, I kissed him gently on the lips and held my little brother tightly in my arms. Both of us protecting each other from danger that was always lurking in our lives.

"Last night you revealed your nightmares and abuse that had been going on in your life. I need to tell you that when I was thirteen years old, and for the next three years, my uncle assaulted me! It took a lot of strength when I got stronger and older to stand up to him, but I did! I know you think that you are still little, BUT you can say "No!" It works!... And, they eventually stop messing with you! I needed to tell you that I had the same experiences that you have had only earlier in life!"

We reclined on the bed, and eventually we fell asleep..

 The next morning, I awoke all alone: Where was Jeff? The sunlight streamed across the bed. I found the soaked red briefs lying on top of his pillow! I knew this wasn't a dream, or was it?

  Arising, I went over to the computer. The monitor showed my screen saver, which was blinking Moonlight Glow. Hitting a key, I found the message that my little brother had written me:

"I hope you enjoyed yourself last night as much as I loved giving myself to you. Love, Jeff."

 I crawled back into bed as the sun glistened into the room through the window. I couldn't have dreamt it: could I? Here was his wet soaked brief.

 Tomorrow will bring more smiles and love.

Soul Mates in the Moonlight

Chapter 5

Tonight is for you.

I showered to clean and reinvigorate my sweaty body. As I stood underneath the streaming water, I closed my eyes picturing Jeff with his long blond hair, soft lips, and smooth silky sexy skin. I grew hard thinking about him. In response, I grabbed my cock and began to stroke myself. The water cascaded around my hardon. With my other hand I reached behind touching my wet ass cheeks. I began sliding a finger into and out of my lubricated wet hole. Lifting my leg up onto the edge of the bath tub, I reached deeper into my sexually stimulated body. My jacking became faster, as I tightened my grip around the head of my hard throbbing cock. All six inches glistened in response to my soapy hand and the water spraying off it.

The clenched right hand fingers around my dick began pumping faster and harder. In turn, my ass cheeks grasped at the invading object. I felt the intruding digit penetrate deep inside me reaching places that I wanted Jeff to touch as well. My legs begin to tremble, while I stood under the shower. Pulling the foreign object free from my ass, I brought it around to my hard cock. Jacking with both hands, as the water hit my chest, I screamed at the top of my lungs and shot a huge load, which reached all the way across the white bathtub and hit the tiled wall. Cum dribbled out of my cock head and fell down onto the tub floor where it washed away into the drain. I eliminated the remainder by splashing water in its direction.

Stepping out of the shower, I dried myself and put on my heavy terry cloth robe letting it soak up the remaining moisture on my body. Then, I went into the bedroom and checked the computer. A message blinked on my screen saying, "I will be there tonight!"

I took off my robe and got into the bed naked under the white sheets. Then, I turned the night table lamp on low and laid my head on my soft pillow, while I watched the air blow the window curtains As the moonlight entered the room and drifted across my bed, my eyelids grew heavy and drooped: probably from the sexual stimulation and/or the shower.

Suddenly I felt movement, as if someone was getting into the bed with me! I opened my eyes to see my naked little brother Jeff climbing into my arms.! I wrapped them around his compact body feeling his sexy smooth skin touching mine. He smelled like a jock that had just played in a tennis match. Our lips met and kissed. My tongue snaked into his mouth, as he explored mine with his hot appendage. Our hands were rubbing all over each other. I ran mine down his back toward his tight small ass cheeks. I could feel his boy cock, all five and one half inches, and press into my groin! My own was rock hard. It stuck outward and thrusted against his cock. We humped each other for what seemed likes hours but, in reality, was just a few minutes. I could feel his wetness and mine coming against our bodies.

I turned my lover to his side and moved up a little over him. I kissed his face, and I licked Jeff starting at his chin and continuing down his neck. Next, I nibbled on one ear and then the other. My hands stroked his hard muscular chest. My tongue traveled down his upper torso to one of his nipples: he began to moan, "Yes, Terry, I love that!"

I proceeded to the other nib while my fingers sensually circled around the first one. He arched his back into my mouth, as I sucked harder on the second nipple, .My lips and tongue travelled lower down his body reaching his defined, muscular abs. I licked each crevice until I reached his belly button. My tongue dipped down into it wiggling in circular motions. Responding to my attention Jeff squirmed around. His hands stroked my head while his fingers interlocked with my black hair.

I avoided the obvious and nibbled around his inner thighs: Little Brother's beautiful strong hairless loins! My lips kissed and licked up and down coming closer each time to his balls. Then, I skipped to Jeff calves sucking on them,

I awoke feeling the heat of the sun on my back. Looking down there was just an empty pillow, but I could smell Jeff! I knew he had been here last night! This had not been a dream! My bed was sweaty and smelled of spunk. He had to have been here!

I got up out of bed and checked the computer screen. A message was blinking in the sunlight saying, " I love you more now than you can ever know Big Brother! I felt so safe and warm with you last night. I will treasure our first coupling forever and a day!"

I typed back,

"Wishing you were here now, but you are always with me in my heart and in my dreams! I love you Little One! Till we meet again, Terry"

Soul Mates in the Moonlight

Chapter 6

By Terry Jeff

Clouds drifted across the sky allowing moonlight to occasionally shine through my bedroom window. I lay naked under my white sheet exhausted from a long day of school and hard work.

My mind wandered to the last time my thirteen year old boyfriend, Jeff, was here. I adore him so much: He means the world to me.

I am attracted by his golden hair, compact size and smooth muscular body. However, it's his big heart that won me over.

 I love his strong hairless thighs which clasp my hard hot cock permitting me to hump him until I explode. He always tightens his legs around my rigid throbbing member, as I move my tool in and out between them.

 My little brother is fully aware I will do anything to please him. .

 Reaching across the bed I felt the cool sheet reminding me he would soon arrive.

 I glanced over to the computer, but the monitor was blank. Then, suddenly, it flickered:

' I will be coming soon, Big Brother Terry!"

 My heart leapt with joy, while I lay on the bed impatiently anticipating his arrival.

Having fallen asleep in the interim,   I was aroused by the combined motions of the lifting sheet and compacting mattress: I looked up in time to see a naked body, my boy's, joining mine.

He leaned over to give me a passionate kiss me on my lips. His arms embraced me, as he lay on my chest looking lovingly into my ocean blue eyes, while I gazed into his.

 He whispered, "How was your day?"

"Long: Because I kept taking out your picture from my wallet to stare at it while dreaming about you! Aside from that, I am doing well: I have high marks in all my courses."

"How are your sports and school progressing?" I added, as he scooted up over my body, pressing himself into me.

"Things dragged in the same way they did for you: I, too, looked at my lover's image and thought about him!. My skill at playing rugby is improving greatly. We won our last game! And, my grades are very good: Thanks to your genuine interest in my welfare. I must always do my best for my eighteen year old boyfriend, so he will continue to be proud of his little brother!"

I reached up to put my arms around my buddy. Next, I hugged and squeezed him.

 We passionately kissed. Pressing our lips hard, our tongues searched, probed and wiggled inside each other's mouth.

My thirteen year old lover's blond hair fell into his face while moving his lips to nuzzle me on my neck. Jeff nibbled down to my chest causing me to violently throw my head backwards with my black mop now sprayed across my underlying pillow,

Using his tongue to lick my upper torso in circular motions, drove his eighteen year old boyfriend crazy with lust. I felt his rigid five inch hardness press against my leg. Meanwhile, my half-footer jabbed him in the belly, as he continued his "rotor-router" activity on my left nipple.

Moaning, loudly, I said:

"Jeff, little brother you know what I like!"

He nodded, as his hand reached up to fondle my second nib. My back arched up off the bed in response to his vacuum-like activity.

He lowered his head running his teeth gently over the outlines of my defined abs developed by all the wrestling and swimming I partake in. His mouth tickled me when it suctioned on my navel, causing me to I laugh out loud. Then, I felt his hand trace a path along the inside of my thighs, playing with the underlying fuzz. Turning his head downward, he made love to my sensitive inner legs after spreading them apart. With his hips near my face I saw how hard he had become.

Leaning over I munched on his smooth sinewy flanks causing him to emit a deep guttural whimper.

Momentarily reaching down, his playful hands massaged my toes before returning his attention back to my thighs. I felt him pull one of my knees up, hooking the adjoining leg with his arm: thus, exposing my tight hole to his onslaught.

He explored my puckered love chute: bathing and, then, fingering it. Pressing his face into me, enabled his tongue to enter and exit my inner being.

I let out another moan, as he continued to worship that area of my body. My right hand snaked down his back twirling his blond hair upon encountering it.

Then, he traveled down to my balls, swallowing one and, then, the other. My steel-like prick twitched, when he sucked on my testicles.

Reaching over I grabbed his smooth cock stroking the tip of it with my tongue. My lips encircled the head, as my hand caressed his hairless balls. I swallowed his tool in one fell-swoop.

That was the instant I jerked my leg out from under his hooked arm, feeling him gobble up the knob of my dick. He was licking it as if it was a lollipop: His tongue traveled up and down the sides of the shaft. My legs quivered while he continued.

Bobbing on his dick, it grew in my mouth. Now, we were passionately making love to each other in sync. My own cock began to enlarge at the same time my ass clenched in and out to his sucking. Increasing his tempo we simultaneously experienced the same explosive feeling in our loins.

Releasing his prick, I shouted: "Let's shoot together!"

Wrapping my lips around his five inches I glided in and out at an increasing cadence. His hairless muscular thighs encircled my head, gripping it tightly. My hips moved up and down in time with his tongue sliding over my own cock.

We both moaned in unison.

Our stiffening bodies started to tremble, as we simultaneously shot into each other's mouth. I felt his sweet tasting cum, which is something I enjoy each time we get together. My balls released a load that filled Jeff's aperture, forcing him to swallow it in gulps.

We sat up in the middle of the bed with our bodies entwined: providing an aura of safety, comfort and fulfillment which arises from being in love.

We kissed tasting each other's cum. Then, we repeated our lip lock.

After coming up for air, I leaned over to whisper into my younger brother's ear,

"I love you, little one, forever and a day.

Tightening his arms around my body in a squeeze, he replied,

"I don't know what I would do without my man to guide me while respecting me for whom I am. I adore you, Terry."

Watching a tear roll down his face, when he said those words, I hugged him tightly for a long time.

We reclined on the bed, as the moonlight crept across the room, falling asleep in each other arms.

The next morning sunshine streamed into my abode. Jeff was gone, but a message on the computer said, 'I will be back, Big Brother, I adore you!

 Jeff'

Smiling, I dressed for another long day at school and the waiting memory of my little sibling: who would reappear when the lunar rays next beamed through my bedroom window.

Love starts with a smile, grows with a kiss and ends with a tear of joy.

Soulmates In The Moonlight

Chapter 7

For many months the full moon. clouds obscured the full moon. The breeze had not brought my friend to me, as a result my heart aches. I love Jeff, as he does me. The computer blinked, and a message flashed across the screen saying,

'I hope to be there tonight with you big brother, Terry!'

As I got ready for bed, I put on clean sheets and pillow cases. I sprayed the room, so it smelled fresh. Finally, I placed an ignited scented candle in one of the corners,

Opening the curtains, I clearly observed the moonlight. I turned off the light then crawled naked under the covers, anticipating the arrival of my lover, pal, boyfriend.

I laid my head on the propped up cushions. My eyes teared from my intense emotions, I couldn't wait for my mate! Dozing, I felt the bed move,... I looked up to see my little bro's smooth tight body next to me.

Leaning towards my head, he kissed me on the lips. Ever so gently and lovingly, his arms wrapped around me, while his tongue explored my mouth. I enthusiastically returned the favor. Our passion for each other was reflected in an endless snogging session, during which we frantically attempted to make up for the period of our separation.

My hands ran down my partner's body feeling his new hard muscles, which had develop from playing sports. The touching of his physique caused me to moan, after which I said,

"I love how strong you feel, Jeff!.... I dreamed of your return since the last time you were here, I am all yours for tonight!"

Sitting up cross-legged, he rubbed my chest then my sides. My six inch cut cock began to swell from all his attention. He caressed my legs, avoiding my aching rod which begged for his attention. His fingers traveled up my thighs to play with my balls, tenderly squeezing one, followed by the other.

I spread my hips to give him more room. He leaned over me, I could feel his breath on my pulsating prick.

His tongue swiped the tip of my throbbing dick head,..., I groaned with pleasure.

His hand gripped the bottom of the shaft pumping it up and down. My member grew more rigid than I remember it ever being, it jutted straight out, away from my body.

His tongue repeatedly encircled the rim of little Terry's head, which drove me wild with passion. His oral stimulation and the warmth of his mouth forced me to raise my hips off the sheets.

The combined smell, originating from the candle plus his masculine body odor intoxicated me, as I reached for his boy tool. I stroked it, making the idol of my admiration both more rigid and tumultuous.

He moved, so I could fellate it in the way he worshiped mine. We were as one. I couldn't get enough of him. He went faster, while he bobbed with increasing intensity. My gyrating ramrod dripped, when he lifted up away from my face.

Turning towards me, he aimed his hot muscular boy butt at my rigid pulsating lance. I watched myself enter him. I grabbed his firm round ass to fortify him, simultaneously he rode my penis.

I noticed his sparkling ocean blue eyes stare at mine, my own gazed up into his smiling face. He was in heaven, enjoying the love making between us.. I could hear grunts, as well as moans, escape from his lips.

All of a sudden his began to squeeze his cheeks around my steel-like member.. He pumped harder descending all the way to the base on each movement.

My body curved upward to meet his downward thrusts. I made love to him the way he wanted, he did the same for me. What a perfect method to express our feelings for each other!

Jeff's back arched outwards. He released a scream I never heard him utter before, it came from deep within him. His pistol shot four gigantic globs of cum across my chest, hitting my face, nipples and abs before subsiding to a drizzle.

While he shot, his sphincter clamped my stimulated iron-like rifle which was primed to fire from his thorough riding of it. I exploded four times within his muscular bubble butted posterior.

I could feel the white love juice squishing around my cock buried inside his defined compact body. I pumped inward and outward driving my engorged arrow deep into his inner sanctum.

He leaned over my splattered torso to kiss me on the lips, saying,

"This is all for you, Terry, I love you dearly, more than you ever will know!"

I rubbed my hands down his back, while I felt the cum on our chests binding us. I held him tightly, refusing to let him go.

I wanted to grip him forever and a day. True love acts that way, sometimes.

Getting up, we showered together, washing every spot of beautiful skin on our bodies. The lathered up soap, slowly disappeared into the drain.

We dried off, returned to our bed, after which we wrapped our arms around each other, We fell asleep, while we chatted about school and our lives.

Those, who feel as we, can never get enough of their partner or know a sufficient amount of what each does.

Often, during the course of a day. I take his picture out of my wallet. I stare at the beautiful boy who loves me for whom I am. In turn, he says he kisses me goodnight when he retires.

 We are there for each other no matter how far the distance, because the moonlight always brings us together.

The next morning the candle had gone out, however the smoke still drifted up to the ceiling. I continued to hear my sheets rustle from when my little brother slept with me. I felt, indeed I knew, in my heart the moonlight was gone. He departed, for now, but would return on many other such nights.

Jeff never disappoints me. He always leaves a message on my computer and comes on the moonlit nights, so we might make love to each other. We shall always do this forever and a day.

Soul mates in the Moonlight

Chapter 8

My curtains were drawn back to let in the evening's moonlight. I checked the computer for a message, but none was there. Then, on the monitor blinked the sentence,

 "I will be coming later, Big Brother."

I crawled into bed naked, feeling the cool sheets on my bare flesh. While I watched the lunar rays slowly invade the room. I laid on my side, my head on the pillow, observing the moon inch across the window, it's soft light surrounding me. Suddenly, the mattress moved, I knew Jeff, my lover, my little sibling, had crawled in. He wrapped his arms around me, holding my body tightly, I felt him kiss the back of my neck.

He whispered, "I missed you, Terry, it's been way too long! I love you so very much!"

Turning to face him, his soft warm young lips tenderly brushed mine.

My tongue searched the inside of his mouth then nuzzled his chin, neck and ear lobes.

I murmured, "The same with me, Little One.!"

We lay, tightly holding each other. We discussed everything that occurred in our lives, since our previous night together: school, sports, and scouts.

Despite our busy existences, our thoughts never strayed from our brother. As we chatted, we ground our bodies together.

Our already rigid cocks touched, we pressed our hips, rubbing them back and forth.

My hands slid down his back caressing his sexy smooth skin. His sports-hardened muscles felt great to my touch.

Placing him face up, I nibbled one nipple, while playing with the other. They reacted by sticking up in the air. I moved my head over to the second one licking it; at the same moment I teased the wet one with my fingers.

 I gave his stomach tiny kisses, until I reached the tip of his hard boy cock. I licked his piss slit; next I wrapped my mouth around its swelling shaft. Lifting my head, I said,

 "I think it's grown bigger since last time!"

Smiling, he murmured, " It always does around you, special Big Brother!"

My right hand played with his hairless balls, fondling plus rolling them. He spread his legs wider for me to continue my exploration. My fingers traveled the length of my bro's inner thigh, feeling his hot sleek soft flesh, my mouth bobbed up and down his hardening prick.

Jeff let out a moan of delight, when I swallowed his tool.

Pulling three-to-four inches away from his rod, I tasted pre-cum, a string of which extended from its top to my lips. I blew cool air across its head, watching his pleasure stick twitch against his abs.

I slid between his legs, as he pulled them up, providing me easier access, I licked from the tip of his shaft to his balls. Taking one, followed by the other, into my mouth, I sucked on them, at the same time my tongue continuously caressed them.

My lover's hand jerked his wet saliva-coated cock in rhythm with my munching on his smooth boy testicles.

Wetting one of my fingers, I massaged his butt hole.

He gasped, and then groaned.

I watched my friend grab his knees; he pulled them up to his smooth hairless chest.

"Terry, take me, love me!" he cried softly. Lowering myself, I licked the length of his sleek strong thighs, at the very moment my hand rubbed down, approaching his muscular white ass. My fingers pulled on his firm cheeks, which widened his clean love chute. I leaned in to lube his tight puckered opening, by tongue-fucking it, in preparation for my entrance of him.

I got on my knees between his thighs. I stroked the wet tip of my hard prick along his crack, he moaned softly. Next, I felt him push out towards me, In reaction, I pressed against his hot twitching hole, which gave my tool easy access. I took time to let my rigid thick dick slowly enter him.

Jeff wrapped his legs around my waist, while it penetrated further into him..

My hands climbed up his abs, on to his chest ending at his nipples. My fingers played with his small taut nibs, as my pleasure stick went in and out.

My lover's sphincter clamped my thick hard cock.

I continuously entered, then exited him, while experiencing his heat. The rhythm of my body pushed my little bro up the bed.

He grabbed my arms, holding them tightly. His head rolled back and forth on his pillow. My partner's sweaty wet hair clung to his forehead, his mouth opened wide, after which it closed, releasing muffled groans. Every time I thrust deeper, he emitted a noise, in response to my rigid shaft, touching that special place inside his young sexy body.

Nothing gave me greater delight than making love to him.

Lowering his right hand to his hard prick, Jeff began to jerk it.

I placed mine on his, so I would be able to jack his shaft with him. It was slippery, leaking a lot.

In response, his abs tightened up, before they relaxed. He raised his head up to mine, giving me a passionate kiss on the lips. His tongue snaked into my mouth, while we lip-locked.

Together we worked his pleasure stick harder and faster. His ass repeatedly clasped my tool; at the same time he raised himself up to meet my dick.

Suddenly, he let out a loud scream; he shot a huge load of cum, which reached his face, splashing his nose, plus his cheeks. Then, a second burst landed on his neck and chest, leaving a trail from his stomach to his boy cock, plus covering our hands.

Grunting, he clamped onto my shaft. Each time he spasmed, I pushed all the way into his tight young body. I shot load after load deep into my lover.

I stayed buried inside him. My arms remained wrapped around his shoulder, while my torso, rested on top of his small sperm-drenched physique.

His seed oozed all over us, when we arose to kiss and tightly hold each other, secure in the knowledge of our deep love.

I felt his hand snake down my back to my ass cheeks, squeezing them and pushing me further into him. My tool remained hard, it continued to release more of my cum into him.

Getting off the bed, I fetched a wet washcloth to clean us. I lay next to my little bro, pulling him close, so we could watch the moonlight dancing across the ceiling. We fell asleep in each other arms.

The next morning, I awoke to find him gone.

The computer blinked a message, which read,

"That was awesome last night, I love you so much, Big Brother! I will see you soon again."

Smiling, I can't wait for the next time. During all my hours, awake, plus asleep, my thoughts are of him, he remains on my mind forever and a day.

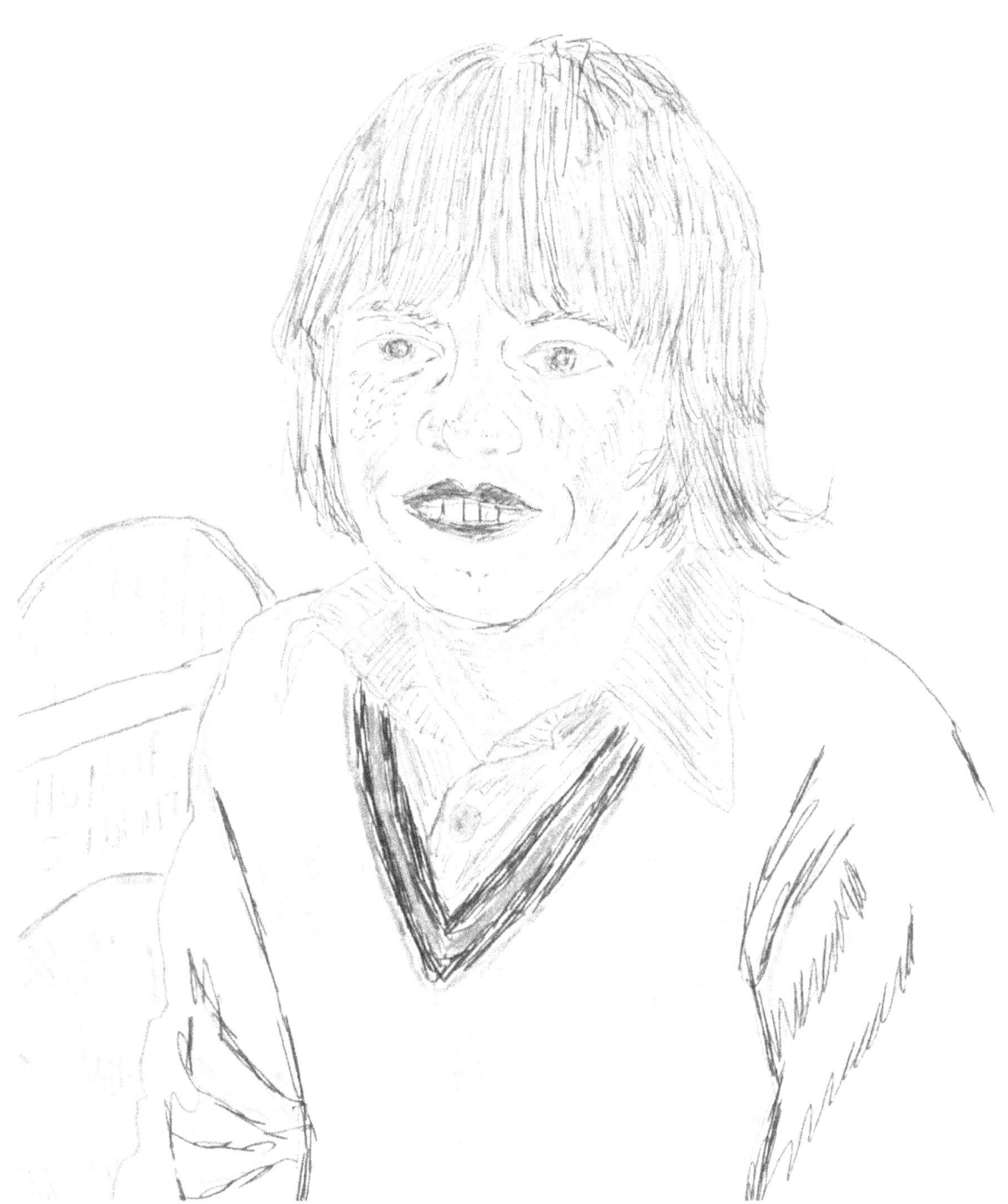

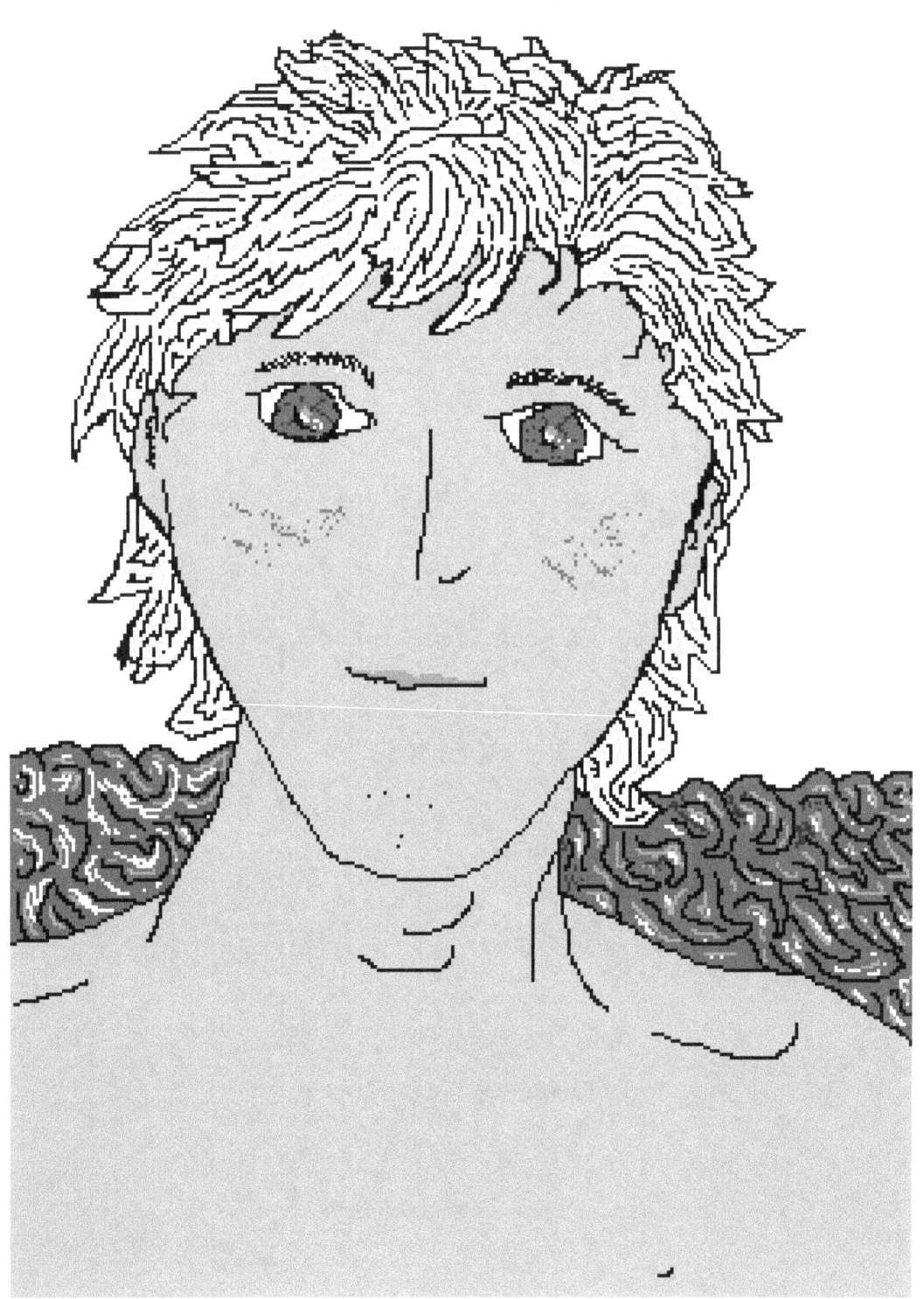

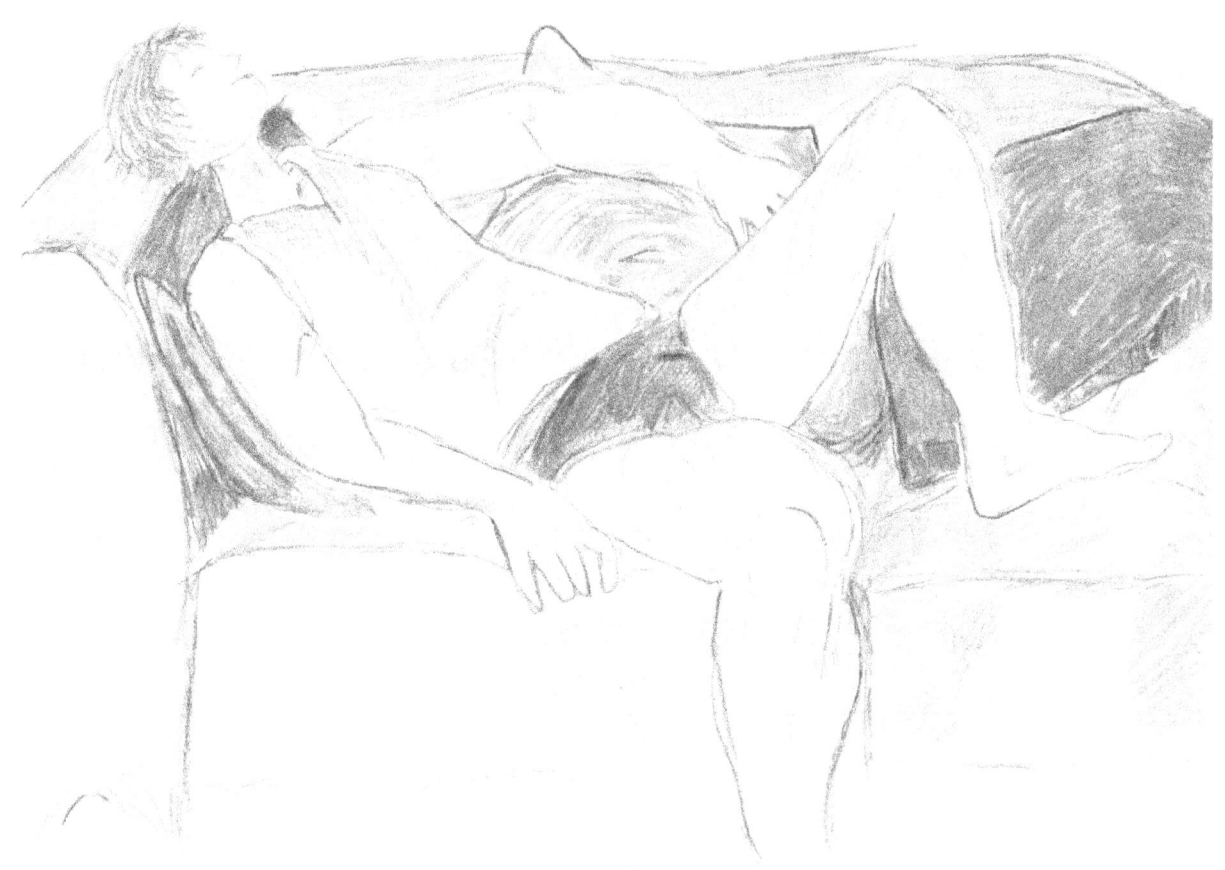

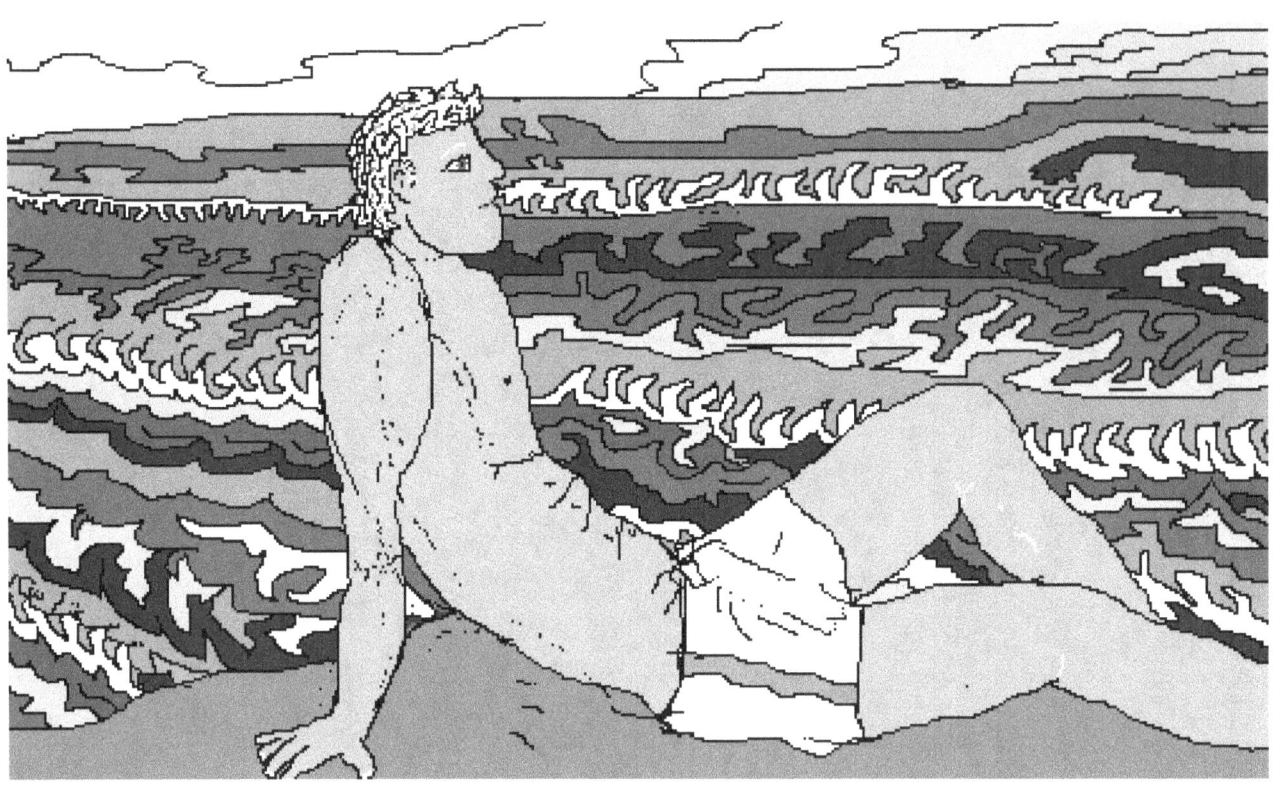

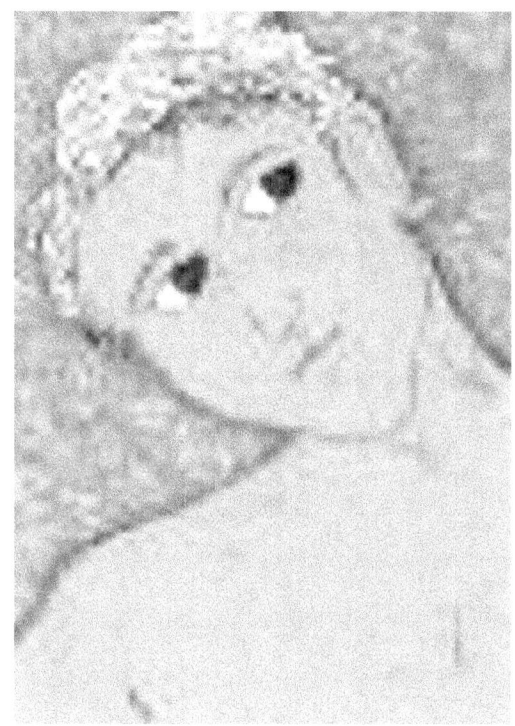

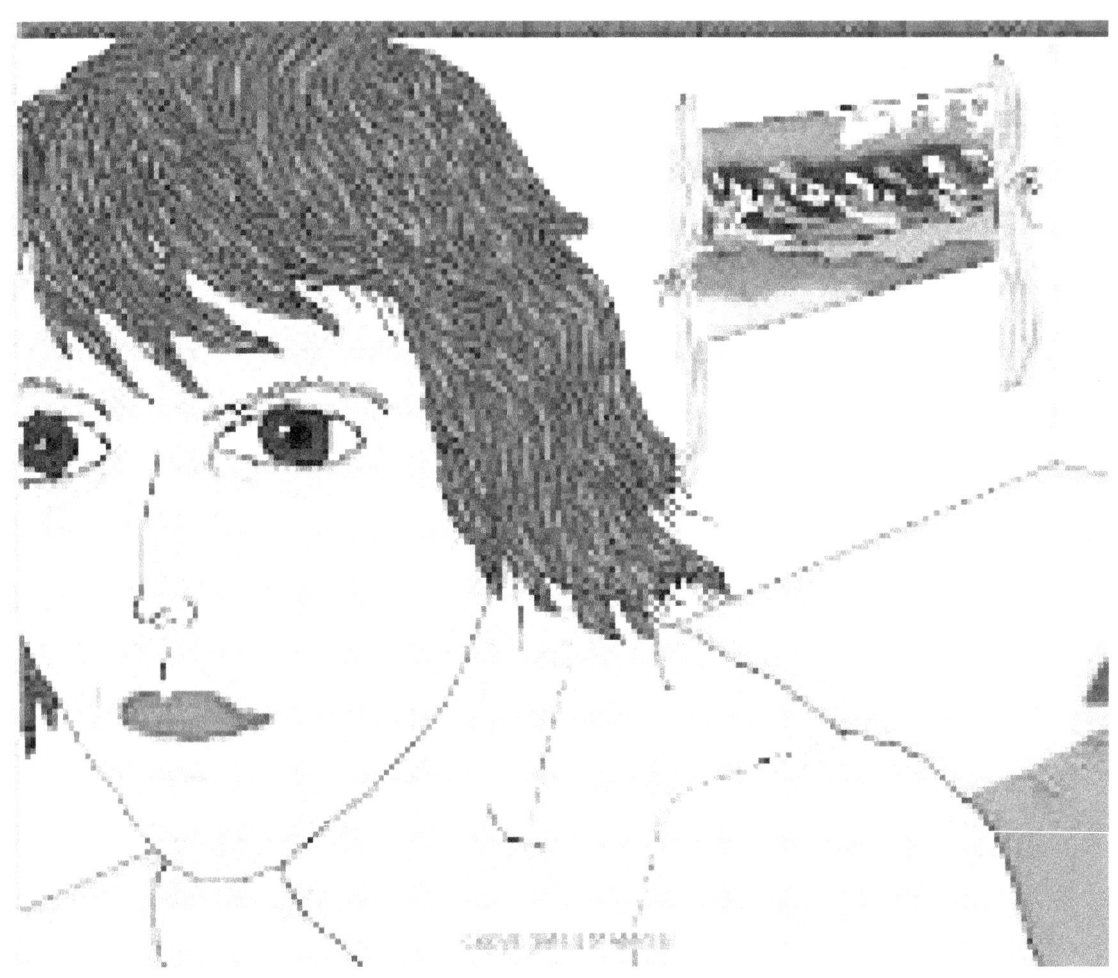

Find your soulmate and love him or her for ever and a day.   Talk things out.   Kiss before you leave. Give a kind words every day. You never know if it will be the last.

I love you   so important that we sometimes forget to say those three valuable words.

gramcontent.com/pod-product-compliance
g Source LLC
sburg PA
31543280526
B00010B/3341